THE LENS-BREAKERS

THE LENS-BREAKERS

JON SILKIN

SINCLAIR-STEVENSON

I AM GLAD TO ACKNOWLEDGE THE FOLLOWING:

Agenda, The *American Poetry Review* (USA), *Antioch Review* (USA), *Bogg* (USA), *Cencrastus*, *Encounter*, *First and Always* (Faber), *Images of Africa* (Wateraid), the *Independent*, *In forma di parole*, the *Iowa Review* (USA), *Kenyon Review* (USA), the *Korean Herald*, *Lines Review*, the *London Review of Books*, *Metaphor beyond time* (UPLI Korean Center), *Mississippi Review* (USA), *Morden Tower (High on the Walls)*, *New Letters* (USA), *New Writing from the North* (MidNag), the *Observer*, *Orbis*, *Poetry Book Society Anthology* (1991), *Poetry Ireland Review*, *Poetry Review*, *Prospice*, *Skoob Review*, *Stand*, *Staple Magazine*, *Tel-Aviv Review*, *Tikkun* (USA), *World Poets* 1990.

A version of a poem originally published by the *Jewish Chronicle* has 'disappeared' into a section of 'Thirst'. *Staple Magazine* gave prizes to two poems in this collection.

I should also like to acknowledge the BBC and their continuing patronage of poetry; BBC Radio Solway, 'A Time for Verse', and BBC Radio Three for the broadcast of a group of poems from the collection; and to thank National Public Radio (USA).

I am also happy to thank the following for their support and generosity in providing residencies:

The American University (Washington DC), Dumfries and Galloway Arts Association (in conjunction with the Scottish Arts Council), Hawthornden Castle, The Isle of Wight Education Authority together with Carisbrooke High School, and the Program of Creative Writing at The University of Iowa.

First published in Great Britain by
Sinclair-Stevenson Limited
7/8 Kendrick Mews
London SW7 3HG England

Copyright © 1992 by Jon Silkin

British Library Cataloguing in Publication Data
A CIP catalogue record for this book is available from the British Library.

ISBN: (hardback) 1 85619 131 1
(paperback) 1 85619 143 5

Typeset by Rowland Phototypesetting Limited,
Bury St Edmunds, Suffolk

Printed and bound in Great Britain by
Biddles Limited, Guildford, Surrey

CONTENTS

URBAN GRASSES   1
FOUR RELATED POEMS   2
'A BLACK HUGE BUTTERFLY'
FLYPAPER
BEINGS
ACHING TO SURVIVE
INTIMACY   5
PAYING FOR FORGIVENESS   6
GYPSY MOTH   9
CIVIL WAR GRAVE, RICHMOND   10
TRYING TO HIDE TREBLINKA   12
JUNIPER AND FORGIVENESS   13
'THROUGH LEAVES AND FRAGMENTED LIGHT'   14
IN TWO SPACES   15
MOSES HARRIS AND THE BUTTERFLIES   16
CHEROKEE   17
INSIDE THE GENTIAN   18
FAMINE   20
ENERGY IS THE BASIS OF MORALS   24
THIRST   25
GRASS CALLED BARREN, NOT BARREN   31
'IF BEFORE'   33
FLOWERING IN WINTER   34
A PSALM CONCERNING ABSENCE   35
FIDELITIES   36
TRANSLATED FROM THE GAELIC   38
IN NORFOLK   40
AMBER   42
WOMAN AND HER BREAD   44
DURHAM BREAD   45

THE LEVELS 47

A MAN AND A PLANT IN A HOUSE 49

PSALMISTS 50

APPARITION 53
DAMAGE
A MAN WITH UNCLENCHED FIST

DOUGLAS OF SORBIE AND THE ADDER 55

GALLOWAY'S RELIGIOUS KILLINGS, AND THE LONELY
LANGUAGE OF GAELIC 57

THE SILENCE 59

GIFTS 61

SEMITE 63

POLISH FRAGMENTS OF DUST 66

TANGLED IN WAR 68

LINKED BY THEIR ACTS 69

JEWS WITHOUT ARABS 71

SECRET SERVICE 73

THE HAND'S BLACK HYMNS 76

MR LLOYD'S LIFE 78

TO A LIGHTHOUSE 79

LENS-BREAKERS 83

HONOURING THE FATHER 86

CLEANING THE LIGHT 87

TENDERNESS 88

FATHERS 89

Urban grasses

With a sickle, I tended the dead in London
shortening the grass that had flowered
on their bodies, as it had in my child's.
And I piled the soil over the paupers' flesh
in their flimsy coffins, which split. What else
was I to do? It became
my trade, my living.

*

Earth, I shall be unhappy to not know
how you go on, when I'm like those
I tended, shearing the grasses
above their foreheads. I felt tenderness
yet I did not know them – and how should I re-assure
that nothing, and say, yes, I care for you
because you are nothing now. Yet you are nothing.
Could I have dared tell them?
and therefore I remained silent.

1

Four related poems

(FOR ED KESSLER, RICHARD MCCANN
AND HENRY TAYLOR)

'A black huge butterfly'

A black huge butterfly, – I stepped
from its lashing progress

of frail sheets, no targets in them, the wings'
brushing circumference, its true gender

from chrysalid to darkness, in the air,
that serene blue fluid; it, too,

indifferent, touching things with darkness,
itself so brushed, those lashing silent metres.

Flypaper

A fly sinks into these adhesions.
Only by tearing a strip of abdomen

or its fiercest organ, the eye, from itself
can it lift away. Us, thieves

of its creaturely flickering wash, the feelers
striking off faeces, the residual

protein, more crucial than its gender,
its face grasping at ours.

Beings

Two minute flies, beings back to back
join with a long black particle.

One of them bigger, its wings raised, holds
both in tension, erect

held perfect connection
for hours, with legs firm over paper

sufficient for them. Their long completion
on white stirs

a single memory, of how
I, too, being with you and by Him

imagined, yet imagining, left
to be, in dire amazed

double shared control
were, on the eiderdown, a feathery creation

of us, palm to palm,
the wings flighted as with joy.

Aching to survive

We fly people, with a fly's hand
clasp fly-like fear, bitter lungs

3

professing care. So, do you mean
kindness, I asked this fly? Scratched me,

the wings unbroken, frenzied
as a butterfly's, a lashing whiteness

from the basking chrysalid, of two flies
tangled, in the sly mentality of lives,

of rasping bosoms that ache to survive.

The frail flesh simulates a caress.
It is turquoise and worry. A slither

of snake-forms in the wings, veins of dirt
whose lashing stills itself. We preen,

for dirt, too, wants its looks. Sucking creatures that fuzz
into the sun, that anxious silent

fortress of light, the good trespass
on a whole fly.

The sad might of minute
life, the tenacious hyphens

that join us in love, in all rearing storms.
So we march to die of each other,

the smell of abomination in combat,
tumultuous vulnerable wings.

Intimacy

I watched a woman feeding
birds, until
my soul went like light: not I (me)
struck on my pulses, but humanity

hammer of light stricken with itself

itself anvil and hammer
hammer and sheet-metal

or, if not it, that hammered
light, not humanity

then you, love, feeding
the menacing forms, their acid hunger.

Paying for forgiveness

In a Trailways, shaking over red clay,
wild poor shapes hang in a sulky wind
of glazed polythene. As we start,
a child bellows softly, she mews at
her mother's breasts pressed up into the v
of an ill-made blouse. The gaze is cheerful,
her repose her daughter's sleep, father
unfolding in it like the soiled shapes
of duster he cannot sell.

The planted rows, the dead all men,
their adversary stain bruised
like mulberry on red clay. A barn
of warped, bare wood pinned in it,
nailed to the shape weather splays. Pines,
their branches held down to gain height
for the bole. The poor lift their arms
and sniff the armpit's sour
compelling familiar. The bus shudders
as clutch and drive engage. 'What's here for me,
the wisp, the grin scratched in a dull pane?'

With a friend, long-tailed males,
gobbling Arab food baked in the fanged
bevelled taste of pine-nuts – taste
of trees in mist – I watched two women
enter the restaurant, the shorter lifting
in the s shape contour of her dress
her silked thighs, like a hind, light
deliberate steps, yet steps full
as the body of a hind as it steps.
'Gentlemen, please,' our guide pleaded.

The engine cuts. Over tarmac
diesel has messed, the journey
unwinds its head like a ball, a twine on which
dead soldiers dawdle
like beads. The lovely energies subdue.
In one hand
the sopping brain
and dead grin, a weed in the other,
its bud in milky blue triangles.

The serpent, none to pick its fruits, creeps
under the bush, to lie up stiff and straight
like a new stick stripped of its bark, coloured
as brilliant as spiced, poor food.
'Hower yawl? I'm white trash (it mimics)
better'n the black.' We grin,
stung like asps, to hear our thoughts
made plain and English. 'How-er yawl?'

Dead and wrong. Those souvenirs, bayonet
and webbing, greed for our fingers. The serpent
shuffles in the bush, the skin, bound to its jaws
in filled triangles of quick shapes
gets stained in blood.

The sepia plates of slaves, the bidding fixed
in their expressions, the flesh exemplary
in servitude. On another plate, mildews
touch the hanging lamp of a rail-junction,
the criss-crossing of rival companies
tracking the prairie, winding the lush anchorages
of lilac brandishing its mourning shapes;
the lamp that grows, the only lamp that grows
solicitude. Like threads a spider runs
across a field, the tracks combine and draw
men keeping farm, or the ashy furnace –

its pour of iron, its granular heat.
Abundant whitenesses of cotton and steam,
their shushed energies serving a head
canted in one direction. They gather
to feed the gatling, poised, bored
on its tripod, ready for the hands to grip,
the face behind it
pieced together, like the seams and cooling-chambers
that make the thing a possibility,
a well-made thing, cunning
as a horse. Like candles, carefully,
firmly strapped to form a barrel:
the grin on triangles, firing blood.

The train has lost the junction, the wagons of men
up-ended in battle, the torn mixtures
of many bodies
hanging from spars, flung against iron castings.
And all the time more pulsing engines sweat;
their heavy boilers, their couplings; the flanged sun.
'How c'n I see yer that ain't he-ah?
We paid reparation until we're white,
to nineteen forty-seven. Now we're fergiven
what yer can't be fergiven of.
For losing a war, like a clip
of a bullet. Ma dear child, the farm
lays in the grass, poverty lays in the grass.'

Gypsy Moth

A Gypsy Moth holds a castle of bruised rose
in its sights, the engine beating like a moth's wings,
but the moths beat against or tumble over
the walls, across beams of light, on glass,
and in the windows – their sensors,
their furred heads, winged bodies with a burning sense
of the bulbs naked over the readers.
Lightly they wipe their webbed flesh
on our cheekbones, and we imagine
ourselves winged.

The Gypsy Moth's self-enchanted drawl,
its music in two notes of self, regarding self,
throbs in the pilot. Satisfaction
secretes over face, mind
and brain, until he is aglow
to do it, to bomb. The readers rejoice
their arrowy targets in the castle tossing spires
through a Gypsy Moth's night sounds.

I hear the Moth on its tarmac, I rejoice
and dream, but imagine death, my head
huge and burned as a moth's. In a field
by the glade furring the gorge, a farmer
sprinkles Shell's nonchalant toxin,
friendless friend, hearing the Esk splash.

Civil War grave, Richmond

This pit is eighteen thousand, where scythers,
uphill, wound coarse grass. A father's kiss
covers the brain of his fifteen-year-old
in a wet handkerchief; the trees' beauteous
philandering grief bursts the sanctuary.

We kiss, we taste a boy's forehead
and our kiss: mercy sees the merciful. And the
victors kiss her hand in a chapel
of wingless moths.
Nothing tarnishes, but kisses: not
victory, not mercy at the
eye of her logic, its futile music.

If you're dead, if you've lost, couth
prayers and silent rifles, are something,
to be flung in a translucent pit,
its jar of suffering. Why

does the body touch us, even
the lopped spiky hand, an elbow's
club, the haunched infantry's shoulder, thorax, hacked
under the nipple? Touch
even these you may not kiss. Brush
them with lilac, and pour on soil.

No smell. Earth soaks it into its musts.

Mercy returns to us, she has altered
her mind, and puts her bony fingers with us
on our arms' hairs; the inch
in thorax, chine, hair and nails,
the eyelashes, of her tenderness, it
is a burning thing to be touched
by her,
and be her ghosts.

(FOR DAWN AND DAVID LATANÉ)

Trying to hide Treblinka

Blessed is the lupin sown to thwart
what our soldiers' hands raised to the light:
a camp with no architectural style,
with a name like this, Treblinka,
and the unnameable, blessed be He, God. *Schlaf*,
as You must, in sleep's grace
of abandoned bliss. And you, God's sweet.
Blessed be He.

Maculate flower.
Blessed the lupin, thick snappable haulm
with innocuous hairs; blessed its noxious seed,
petals, a bird-shaped milky blue.
Blessed the lupin, with no mind to choose a soil
but what sustains it, and what flowers
its unending ignorance. The animal God,
this salmon-spawner, blesses.

The camp, a hole in the eye; its zone, the flowers' assart.
A hill swells with breath and flowers: some blue,
some faded blood ones, that sink their roots
in shreds of carbon made visible
with hours of damp archaeology. Unappeasable
the claws, as they travail
that earth their hands trowelled.

(FOR JON AND ELAINE GLOVER)

Juniper and forgiveness

God unfurls the atomic cries
of arrowy birds. The land smells,
pulling apart tenacious waters.
It is re-creation. Noah gathers to his body
the tender Father's, pushing out
the sprigs of hopping Juniper, 'go, go on,'
through swarming grass.

It is a new earth, and I like it,
with everything that steps from this ribbed ark. Through
    adhesive
layers of air, one integument
breathing with another, shade struck from Ararat
darkens the trees that hurl between grass.
These lacy leaves. 'Attend to us,' they beg;

'yes yes, we are going to.' God's pairs of us
sly and connubial from the old zones,
with a rustling, delicate sense of children.
In sin we see a new vision, leaving
in twos, taking as we must
the smell of Juniper and forgiveness.

'Through leaves and fragmented light'

Through leaves and fragmented light the cricket flakes
her shaped notes off wings. Crouching
by a woman in pain, in the hair on my arm,
on wood, or its faecal ash, she has made visible
the idea for a spring hardened to tear, slowly
apart, our bodies. She is not
that idea: a contralto, her oily discs twanged
into our lives. If what it is
to make pain, what more

to clash this soft battering consequence, lyric
percussion, a pebbled
softly rattled water, that unfastens the two selves
of one mind, to stiffened facing flighted wings.
I search for, find your body-sound
flickering winter in ash's doldrums, the atomic drowsing
in a hearth. And with you
waiting is remembering, where none need
rise in the dark. Tell her, it is so.

(FOR MARGARET AND MICHAEL MOTT)

In two spaces

One space death sledges holes through, and this other
nurturing our exchanges, breath and touch,
that impregnate the sufficing space. But how?

As I worked in London, and shovelled
loose earth over the flowered coffins, I felt

that the dense space, its substantiation
made with the grasp

of limbs endowed with taking from each other,
stayed unrelinquished. Uncertainty
like ice has covered this.

*

Space, with the holes death sledges. In you step
to a different space – a chair and a bed –
breath and touch substantiate. So here

are both spaces, neither relinquishing the other,
swirling translucent wrestlers. How could I

with leave-taking embrace your coming in
this room? Like blood, the space with life
clasped in it enters this impure world.

Moses Harris and the butterflies

'what can thought but devour object and self'

Butterfly and stone, in shade's calico
disguise each other. This ghost-catcher (we eat ghosts)
tenses net and desire. She rises alive
but mistakes, surrendered as Job
to Satan is she to him, with her God's gold moons.

He depicts his trade: 'what I do
is not who I am.' Yet in his nets more tensile
than sea, unless weight
is strength, her wings flummox and tear.
No end, he gasps,
to the times she must be beautiful – like love
catching in the nets.

So this tender fake of beauty
treads with yammering noiseless pulse, etches
a pin, and presses it in the mid-stream
of a moth's thorax. The spidery fur
and fluid nick with air, its sharp
inaudible rush a snatch of dry odour
in the chest.

By a feathery pool
of beasts considering God's dream of mild hinds,
he shoulders aside a branch, enters a silent quarry
of cyanide and zinc, God's uneatable delights.
His airless creatures lay out on slabs. See off the ghosts,
Moses, Moses Harris, you, depriver of wings
and you, deprived.

Moses Harris, an eighteenth-century lepidopterist, produced a book of butterflies and
moths called *The Aurelian*.

Cherokee

On sandstone, barite
makes sand-roses, cabinets of them
in a year of dying. Close, but not close
in kinship, so as to keep those they love
in sight, in the world
next to this, distant
as the odour of plums tossed
in summer wind. The blades of sand-roses
glint, as if touched by mites. They gasp, and smell
of bituminous air. They were
the Cherokees, their drops of blood
made stone in God's washing tears.

They open and don't breathe
in the air's
generative lulls. Wherever mercy
is human, don't look
to pity to come like a child
weeping its maternity, perfect
between the hands of the rushing form
of the Shekinah. Creation is
an Indian fury, needs art for its pain,
statues of hurt.

I smell frankincense, pity's herb.
We'd do right
to be scared of it. If I want
another's sacrifice it must be I need
pity manifest. With little faith
I chafe my hands; tenderness
rubs perfumed between them,
the best, most weeping of grasses,
the least form of life I crop.

Shekinah: the female principle of the deity in Judaism.

Inside the gentian

This gentian is paint, its form
seeping in coarse paper. Off the anther float
the pollens, mysterious wingless
birds of fertility. Veins of damp thread
stitch its flesh. This is the size of magic,
a deformation of spells: the petals
sudden and huge, their slender cliffs and space
with birds in them, stiff as pencils,
the teeth clenched, the pubis trailing in a sac,
gold discs of pollen a guano of unmelted frost
on their quills. In the gorge a glow rises
from the self buried in its anguish
of self-hatred. Its cat's teeth bare,
its false matrimony of self with self
a wet clinging garment. Find another's face, for eyes
and light would beg for blinding
if your smiling had no hand
to touch its mouth. Above me,
voices, a parliament of indecisions
like animals with no speech,
its grammar, its voice and pitch
violent, as if for murder. I hear
in the faint percussions of the stream
a brass band, to their necks in mud and water,
a regiment with our *absentia*
scratched on their bullets, their arms raised
with rifles. These lives pell-mell,
with extinction certain and distant as light
in the satanism of night's indigo.

We stand in the fickle dome of light. Where are the fruits
in their preserving straw? In the hands of the blind.
She put them there.

Praise the gentian, her gravid form
for the printer more visual than a kiss
the hand, its brush of eager pigment
the printer's blocks, his adhesive inks
and the platen's waiting tray.

Praise the gentian. Praise her.

(FOR RODNEY PYBUS ON HIS FIFTIETH BIRTHDAY)

Famine

The dips of this mountain, mild as her back's hollows
have barbs of moss in splintered quartz. Three luminous
    peaks,
close, like tines. Dabs of coarse wool, on paths
that hold the pastures fat sheep tear, as if
the grass would starve back to the pebble it
    has split.
A dead fox, its mouth of saw's Vs, the ants
are sawing off her neck. Someone who'd caught her
had trussed her back legs with stiff, wax-like cord
of nylon, used for tying sacks – their cruppered shapes.

The cruelty is palpable and simple
the fox's teeth jagged as glistening rock
the fox's mouth open with pain. Yet God fills
the parted air, the helmet of foliage, and requires
His clay creatures, at play with animals
models of His designs. We kneel: his grief
is sudden downpour
we're sopping with. His tears make iodine
tracing our acts, staining the print scratched by
a kidney stone, small and blunt as a match-head.

The trapper, that little one in Yankee plaid,
his mouth, its collusive decipherment
of what is vulnerable, has ceased its mirth.
The lips in strata dried like a shale, half mud
with a tobacco stain, and poverty.

I see chevrons on the milky herring, their blemishes
traced in salt. You drift, and I with you in tilted seas.

*

He cut water and mud. This was creation,
Ireland, its pudgy apple blossoms roughing
each other, like tribes.
Curoi Mac Daire, with a body white as death,
has spread warrior thighs. His son's face
tilts with regard, taut smiling mouth
watching his father's sword cut the softness
of cow-parsley. His wife is Blathnaid,
has hair never unplaited, and hugs
a bolster, made of flock from their sheep,
hot and belligerent.

She esteems Cuchulainn. He's like a thistle,
a flower that slakes her, its mineral nut-like juice.
He lifts her husband and her son – the long blade,
the bodies, screaming. Where, she asks, in the world
will tenderness, a lingering female god,
be again?

With feathers greased, limbs pinned back for long
   flight,
the air behind in oiled streamers, they lift up
their wings in sexual preparation, tiny swimmers
inside a howling, and a scrupulous space.
She, he, him – arrow-shape, containing
the druid that her husband cared for. He preferred
all three: Love to his Lord – meat, bed, and fire.
His wife, her wit – its sweet sheer taste of her smiling.
The boy: because he loved him, future lord
of his experience and tutelage, his winter's bee
in a small exposed hill-fort. He leaps, with her
in his arms, off a cliff. They lift,
the breakers, the bashed green turtle rocks,
the mottled treacherous blood splintering
in algae. White warmth and red hair
tangle with daylight,

the light in curls, flesh straight as a stripped stick
is white.

*

The tribes, like blossoms roughing each other,
let in the Danes, bringing their prow-heads, cut
in delicacy and ferocity.
Then comes a Norman face, his metal nose
fitting his visor, the chest's width armoured – no part
uncovered, but a hand, white, tapered,
pointing a sword. His frame
is slender, and trained as a whippet's.

*

Grasses rub the furred necks of horses, their joints
large with succulence and flexibility.
Behind the half-circles of gates, England's pasture, Ireland,
her soft wealth a fleece, a thread,
as if from God's strong hair. The Gael
has a huge obsolescent head; it tilts
to the Norman's willowy stick.

Mild Gaelic chews its delicate address
in diphthongs, worries at its survival – shall it,
shall Gaelic, die . . . be as spit
in the futile grey of the Atlantic's?
Their uncomely hands face upwards. Rain is it,
or grace? In a flaking sun, creatures;
in a moist air, their steamy forms: pink mouths
with delicate froth. Some pray nearby, where the cut fields
have rows of heads – men who watched spears of grass,
and the calves of herdsmen pricked by them, and saw
their dewy infantry. This is Cromwell,
England's soldier.

When he has found the trembling hare, its silent gasp
in a shook, or last triangle of standing wheat,
he scythes the fields, again, he hugs mountains
where the god's a shielding stone, and rain's poignant arrows
scratch the cliff, lapsing in a lake of black and rose.
I tremble with the height. Below,
a boat, its stone hull
upturned. With praying under it.

*

Chapels in the grass's time, themselves blossom, with primroses
and straggling vivacious eglantine, like wire. Their flagstone
notches the sky's blue, a slate bruise-colour,
and hasps a ring to heave it up with. Were the saints
for to suffer our suffering? This it seems

we asked for: generous blood in the heather,
lanterns of it on stems, blobs of litany.
Music hidden like a hare, their two lines of singing,
a double hymnal of men with women, a paired foliage
of pliant acanthus. Praise us,
for surviving, greedy for our neighbour's love
to the touch precious as bread, the moist
dead sustenance.

FOR KEVIN AND TRISHA FITZPATRICK

'Shall Gaelic die?' A poem by Iain Crichton Smith, written in Gaelic and translated into
English by the poet.
    'The grass's time' is a phrase from a poem by Jon Glover.
    Curoi Mac Daire was a chieftain who held a hill-fort on the Dingle Peninsula in south-
west Ireland. His wife, Blathnaid, betrayed him, and her lover Cuchulainn murdered
both her husband and their son. For good measure they took with them the household
druid but, loyal to his Lord Mac Daire, he took Blathnaid in his arms and leapt with her
off a cliff.
    Cuchulainn: in Gaelic literature, chiefly the *Ulster Cycle*, this Irish warrior of pagan
times figures as a great hero of legendary feats, and is sometimes described as 'the
Achilles of the Gael'.

Energy is the basis of morals

A stag tears the lilac horizon. His fear
compounds the energy of dogs. He billows

as they leap, and subsides, his spine kicking
in the torn lungs, master smiling, 'eat.'

He has starved his creatures. His webbed gums
large with blood and saliva, the sud crushes

on blaeberry lips. His dogs consume the creature.
I tear my soldier's khaki, its opals

of blood, and stitch leaves for my body
because the Potomac reflects me naked

and I want the dignity and insolence of nature's clothes
on me as we kill. I have seen

my father stoop and swill the frail marble
of his shoulders; my soldier's blood runs,

'dead,' I hush to myself. As I feel
men's thighs exalt their horses, I ask

what grains the xylem, what selves
the gene in the harming, mystic blood.

(FOR BILL AND ANN DARR)

24

Thirst

1 *Gratitude*

With a mouth of glowing mist, the harvest moon
urges our silent voices, body-dew,
damping the hammer-beam with soft, bat-like
nocturnal hymns. We thank Him for the grain;
its short fractured energy
like broken-up lightning. His harvest's metal hook
feeds our mouths.

These are silenced voices. But by them
a forest, its howling speeches; cones thrash
past branches. A thief alerts: his jacket tight
on his chest, like bark. He bashes old dismal lives
for brass. Yet this is the time to stray through houses.
Our doors hang ajar; cut in the balusters
hearts beat with gentleness, through which a cat
noses dried honesty, stemmed in a vase.
The back lane cries for rags and fur; fierce as ginger
he treads, in the currant bushes hung
with his piss. We must thank ourselves
who are alive.

No no! gratitude's the way, touch God's virtuous mouth
of herbs, the bashing circuitries of seeds.
Slyness filches to the forest-raspberries,
by imitation, the grass's lightning.
His admiration is a mouth of leaves.
He glares his black lamp; thief.

2   *Praising*

We praise the harvest, a swirling helix of leaves
stuffing each other's mouths, gentle tornado
of glut. Gratitude bites the underpart of God's mind.

3   *We are cared for*

Energy, jagged clinging force, lying in
the thief's first life, chose a priest's.
Small lower lip, sensual
large upper one. A little mirth soldered
to the corners, plural vulnerable delicacy,
like a leaf grazing another.

The passover salts them together. One man is,
and the other, said to be a god.
A finger-nail dips in salt. This is Judas,
not a Judas yet, touching
Christ's fingers, kissing his moon-lit cheeks;
the light of the world will char his soul.
Christ shouts, 'I've chosen, Father,
but will You melt to an uncorrupted
strategy of light?'   Judas's lips
dry as silver.

The oval heads of nails, hammered to unnatural
duty, fleck with blood, and weep
in Christ's wrists. Their shining is over. Envy tears
the mind's salad, Judas destroys his body;

and earth renews its cruel gland. The priest cares
for us, to the ends of the earth.
He draws a line

over water, without termination, his vessel fleeting
in seas bifurcated by the polar cap.
His strong adhesion is to pairs of us.

4   Green wind

Green wind shakes open the trees' heads, their isolate
voices, a tissue of moaning
in unbrotherly solitude. This is the harvest-time; be
   rejoiced.

5   Good chance

Work out what to carve, between mind and the fractures
in the butte's snowy happening. Stand and smell
the wind off its corners. From the noisy grass,
twin-tracked by tyres and feet, be fortunate,
pick up the horseshoe, its thrift of motion.

6   The way we choose to live

His people thought they were his progeny.
Their praise, shaking upwards like smoke, he deflected
to their God. No sacrifice in blood;
they choose, litanies with mashed herbs,
an oblation of leaves. Even this they regret
but sense God requires something. They provide
no pacification of brutal godhead.
Thunder is a goddess. Tears are ours.

Their elegance, a modern gratitude,
a thankyou in their mouths, the leg sturdy
on its considerate heel, the instep's tenderness.
In the yearly tabernacle, a trembling horn
ushers in the hoped-for forgiveness.
'There never was a promise broken,' she whispers
to her husband, 'but was redeemed in pain's
massive later time.' The judging, tremulous horn.
The halcyon ark bobs in the steps of
one with a mind for God, spittle flecking
a mouth of pride. He kisses his fingers
and touches this disrobed sacredness, as it
flings by. The priest flowers his prayers
over the year.

The hems of the acts that lift the scroll
to the congregation swish the chosen one.
'We must have forgiveness,' they shout. 'You have it.'
He unscrolls leaves, sewn, not for nakedness,
but vulnerable words, prancing before God
like children, uncertain if to be grateful
or independent. The fig-like mind
fleshes with trembling, its hopeful generous seed
proud if it dies unsolaced.

I lie half-dead in a tug, that smokes like a man's
dark, furious pipe, in the Ohio's sluice,
beating nightfall with pudgy disdainful wings.
Slow, thorough, the bastard Charon.

Take heart: the last this body sees, 'Oxo,
good for the brain.' I die, advised.

The priest gathers the wasting languages
spoken by a handful of fingernails.

7   *King Hezekiah, the spring, and a water-tunnel*

Night's dim herbage tense and feeding stiffens,
like creatures lifting their mouths, with fur beaded
in surprise and water. Hezekiah kneels, cupping his thirst.

If water tastes thirst, if sweetness finds
thirst's shifting delirium, if it is sweetness
as much as thirst, how is it thirst resists?
If thirst is water, it must show disdain,
except for dry mouths. Hezekiah drinks
as if he would die: the amused water spills
pink solitary thread. To tame thirst,

to have and quench it, with pipes that thread
water through his house; the cats mew
at doors, for portions of religious meat.
This whole sufficiency, this was modern
this modern water, its sufficiency.

Yet water springs away, untamed. Cut thirst's
obdurate highway through the flaking mountain; turn,
biblical water. Don't stop, or be poisoned.

The city's families, in loops of aching rags,
cloth subservient to the day's thrift, wait
for the king, to surprise, to garland them with promises
of liquid: thirst stands, in flowing water,
imagining it passes through the rock,
its linked fingers
of liquid concatenated,
pursed and braided small puissant spring
headed for rock. 'Say it,' the stone tells him.
'I say it,' Hezekiah, unused to mountainous talk.

Water springs off its coil, insects fuzz
the sun, Hezekiah, seeing the plan,
their thinking, how it concentrates like leaves
shaded on each other, concatenations
of taken light,
dilapidation of winter leaves
shedding summer's thirst, shadow hanging on wood,
densities of wood and leaf,
an upward darkness piercing the light.

'Shall I be soused in sweetness, they in their loops of rags?'

The entanglements of grass with earth, and beyond
the stain of water, salt chevrons of sand off the herring.

'Water,' he says. Agreement swarms like a fish.

Hezekiah, twelfth king of Judah, diverted the spring Gihon by tunnelling through a hill,
thus bringing the water to within the walls of Jerusalem.

Grass called barren, not barren

It bows lacelike barren heads, it is not barren;
its seed, short fractured energy
like broken-up lightning;
a scent of forest raspberries wipes the grass awns,
my mind stores their lilac's softer scratch.

*

The cost of giving, is giving more.

Dead nations, their mouths bitten by hunger:
in mine their ventriloquism suppliant
as a chained cat, the tether
of his spurting cries.

Heads bloom in their ancient coins;
on the obverse, seed wedges in the crook
of three awns, like supple, nonchalant
kicking legs. The people's bread, goddess, their sex
    therefore.

Dead sex, in billowing forms scratched
in the brothel wall
you step through. You are intense. The amber
you wear glows on your daily nakedness.
By taking thought, you can make a child; as simple
for you as the man lifting a shell
to his armour-piercing weapon in its turret.
His tank is hit: its iridescence peels
like webs of broken light.

You give birth. Your sex has nothing to do with it,
the opening of heavenly flesh. Five stars harness

their plough hid in flagellant, pulsing light.
Your hand is stiffening
its milky palm the outlay of female giving.
A man's love is tender in you,
you fill with humanity, blessed grateful goddess.
In place of our sacrifice, you adore us.

*

By imitation, the raspberry filches
the broken-up lightning of the grass-seed.
Grass will have none of the fruit: it is a pure self
that knows its acts, and magnifies none.
It is its gnosis, the secret soul
that dies in immaculate completion.
Your grass my flesh touches, sensitive goddess.

Woman of grass, if you are generous,
I shall prick in the coin's fecundity –
those bashing circuitries
held in the seeds on a nation's penny –
a bullying comma. The reverse side is king.
Goddess, bless me,
in my having been alive, although I can't lose that.

'if before'

If before it were surface
now it is not, with you,
and I felt it was still deeper that it must be
as the plane roared passively
in the tolerant spaces, these iced blue clarities;
afterwards the aircraft murmured,
but that was not too late.

If fanaticism, the little dust of madness,
a dust
like the aircraft's burnt mineral on snow,
if love does not dare willingly
like the eyes of politics, its assent,
or grow of itself.
I care, love.

She put him in and he
began that long, exquisite journey of mutual satisfaction.

Flowering in winter

I cut winter flowers for a stone jar
hoping to hear from you: two of each – heartsease,
with faces like the twittering dial of a compass,
its magnetic tenacities
filamenting ships, in water bifurcated by the polar cap –
and the five tab-like petals of jasmine
children leaning through a carriage window –
I sifted in the stems
of winter blossoms, the wind's hurrahs
tearing like the ends of hair, to flowers.
The asymmetric aggression
breaks into harmlessness.

Where are your words? your face
unpetulant as dew. You hope for the best,
and bud as constantly as the moon. I put my hands
up to your cheeks, the flower
of our hurt, for fear to touch
you elsewhere, the bud precious between sepals:
my hands, your face. There will never
not be the moon, flowering a man's hands.

But love, its dignity! The moon, her mature
belly, is a Jew wandering the night sky;
his gold is beaten to her silver. Her light's a forceps
she gives birth to ships with, tridents that crawl
over her livid heaving face
of sea. Is it sorrow?
The extreme of love. Go on. The tides whamming
against the vessels they raise:
it is love, it is.

A psalm concerning absence

The glade is an eye, a dense unseeing space
holding that preciousness, absence.
The heavy trees have their thinness,
the leaves, the jagged swivelling ovals.
Shanks of birch
have untangled muscle, untapering widths
constant as this absence.

The lucid forest eye hangs blind
as the huge, feeling elm. Nor can bough or twinkling leaf
make this eye blink, or the eye hanker
after a trail through firs
mixed with autumn's deciduous mist.
Through the twittering mosses

rises merriment's smiling lip,
wide sheer cheekbones, and teeth
your smile quick at my stag's heart. The hand
sheds its touch constantly. This this, flutters the bird.
Please, I want my hands at your face
that flowers bewilderment, in whose midsts I beat
my male wings into the thicket.
We are the animals devouring absence
and the humans that transcribe it.

Fidelities

She stewed the plums now
that in the tree's plenty
we might have some in the
winter when there's none

Climbing through a soft tangle of spring growth
the air fennel prints is hard to breathe;
I climb further slowly. She's not here
the sexual scent off my screens. But brick-smells
and tar, like cold in a tooth's nerve.
And the sea's tangs – fish, petroleum,
and the horn of a liner, its cabin-pricks of lights,
the hot joyous worlds, or money and dissatisfaction,
dance-music; nothing I can touch. The captain's smarm
touches off romance. A half-bared shoulder.
The sugary ooze of plums, a cool taste
hot in the pans. The girls are held
at their thighs by the v-shape pleats. You tasted
the honey. You fucked, and I didn't.
I didn't choose, and you did.
Treachery comes out of the sea
like a goddess, her fur is dark
as the mouth of a fish. Sea-smells
in the dawn's cobalt and pink. And the soft-smelling
    complication
lining everything. The starched, empty sheets.
Running to a hole, the water wrinkles.
It is a question of unfaithfulness,
the promulgation of light in her hair
the designs of sex, the steps up
into fulfilment.

            The sea's drying waves,
cake-like apartment-houses
of both sexes, and the slithering torsions
reflected in windows, the menace
of evening pleasures, deck chairs bent double
in anguish against rain –
the soft smell in itself. And finally.

Like a blunt nib the bus tugs
from its inkwell a contour
of wavy road between cliff and sea.
And fumes drop after it
a smutch of powder. Powdered gas.
A spiked undulant and the railway
enter the smoking cliff – its space, a dull odour
of electrics. Which stall with a number
do I piss in, what disease pollinates
its sticky, star-shape plasm in this hall?

Italy rejoices: the pumiced glimmer here
of release from the German clasp
forty years earlier, when I saw a soldier
refuse a man water. Everything
that is War is evil, they tell us.
Do we speak? the clever
are the quiet ones with no harm
in their syntax, who whisper into chambers
where the living catch fire (it is untrue;
we burn gas and paper). Faithful to all victims
but her, my mind murmurs. Beware the unfaithful
hungers, and the wispy hilarity,
the trenchant clinging odours, a smell of water.

Translated from the Gaelic

From where he was born on the island of Harris he lives
fifty miles, which, across the water, is so near you might
plough there. But this is brine anxious for blood, so that to
be near is not to be close; although this sleeve of sea can
sink its fractures and lie guileless in placidity.

Whenever you turn to watch him, he is facing away from
the island, its old geology which gave him as a child some
joy, and permitted the midnight sun to have its woman's
bony fundament. Lord, the island is many witches, laid
one upon another. Yet even the lightest wind might bear
him home, although that would be premature and
mischievous. Look what I've done, it might say; and
surprise would fire the abandoned labradorite, as
unusable as sadness, although its blue was once the
weight braking the ship's scudding velocity, a ballast of
laminated gleaming prodded up in the cratered vicinity of
Hudson's Bay.

Strange blue grin. He, too, would be surprised by the
wind's acts, and his protest would sound like those voices
spraying across each other's psalm, which the precentor
initiates, its laudation the parabola of distance without
measurement. Perhaps; for the region's unkind theology
has instigated a secular mind in a religious being. He
knows that the soul, in, or after, death, or even before it,
may be filleted by a priest's after-dinner rancour.

And how will those without teeth and situated in hell, he
asks me, wail and gnash? Teeth will be provided, he sighs
lightly. The sigh is a prism. What he smirked at is a part of
some unimpedable yearning. The prism is a sextant, the
sextant an astrolabe, which before that was instinct.

Which is what it is now, and he could home over water with instincts like Trojan soldiers forcing Greeks into trenches of spikes. But in that first home the God of rationality sells ten to hell for every one predicated on heaven.

His wife understands every fragment of this, and laughs. Stark sunlight blesses his life. A foliation of archaeology enriches it. Shall Gaelic die?

FOR IAIN CRICHTON SMITH

In Norfolk

The yachts graze. With long necks that stoop
to crop, they suffer us
as their teeth stain in grass. Frugal hands sort bricks
in a sandpit, their utility, heft
hue and shapeliness, broken. Two fields link corners
above it; the owner stands like still wind,
with his daughter, her sensitive gold. The white barley
a collective of old men
with hair lifting, he touches her. She will mate
a Nelson,

the girth of Norfolk's stags. His men steer wide horses,
their intelligence wastes
in petrol, as they plough
v-shape screams of birds. 'Magic,' they smile
as their children stare,

and the stars drop on their tables one night
a month – Orion's disentangling silver.
But they're harrows, knuckles smashing clods,
in their eyes
meteorite flints.

And as they die their houses suffer
not the soul's brief flit – but this, a shunt
to a builder's pit. It's here, in their pitch
of scent I can't sense, the nettles
entangle butterflies, a cloudy opal that dusts
my eyes; the lepidopterist, a male
venus, nets in his desires.
I smell houses broken; a nimbus
of humid fertility
in pools; and the half-used life

of the prodigious cross-beam wastes
diagonally across the pit. In my hands
is shoddy mortar. 'Uh,' you say, its dusts
on the long plaza-shapes of your foot and instep.

We are twittering birds, we'll beat our wings
out of this; the prospect is a fragile scent.

Amber

In Poland, pines
blob their moulting pitch-like sap
into the salt: fossil, fossil gum,
a resin the State lifts
like intense, red fish.
Intimate elegist of
life's raw, Catullus grafted
into his mind,
like a wort,
a staunch, for the soul's bleeding,
the love that pained him, the stippled
fluttering wings that found
a sparrow's warmth
in her breasts. I've threaded
a chain with this amber.
This little wear-thing,
round-the-neck garment,
its loop and comma, will indent
the left of your right breast
and the right of the other.
Dandle this substance, that's slow to warm
but warms right through, its flow
hardened in salt,
between your breasts.
Not that,
like hands round a sputtering match
I don't want mine
to hold you, but that
when I take them away, this pine's drop
will touch you, not
like a sparrow, but with
this other warmth I say
is mine: but is

the amber's, this rubbed
electric that will
limber alien
compatible energies.

Yet if nothing threads us,
like beads pierced
on cotton, keep this alive
substance as token, as warmth,
as if we were
to have had love.

Such as five pelted, shivering
almost unclothed
Welsh saints found one night,
in Pumpsaint. Not love, but a warmth
nature's bitter soulless hands
could not take from them
that night, as they sheltered
their heads on stone.

An inn. Refuge smoulders
a chimney in
this watered valley,
this Welsh paradise before
England cantered
horses over it.
The river Cothi turns
straight from the farm. I touch your mouth.

Woman and her bread

What I cared for was not bread, not,
in our road, a van's doors pulled back to feed
hunger, but the two, inextricable, with men lifting
panniers, whose days were also youthful.
I was glad for the man's smoky breath caught
in my boy's jacket, its forked gender
of economy on my girl's body.

I'm cheerful, and inspect
the day's loaves like fishes, hundreds to feed the thousands
old as me – a peg, rammed,
and split, on a clothes-line, with garments flapping
like married lives in a violence
fire exceeds. Is this the jubilee
of each day's bread he bequeathed me? This
it is, and I'd bless each loaf
lifted inside the shop, for the till's medals
and tabs to rise, on the day before yesterday
is shorn of its lamb. I'd die of bread,
its pitted textures, its magmas
of dark confectionery. It reminds me, baker,
of you. You rose early,
and died, the cross of this morning,
its wood to be assembled, for the day
to be the day it is, not yet
put together. Although, surely, goodness and mercy

will come to me in the next life. I love you,
baker, and hope to see you. If I clasp
my youth's joys in age's adoration,
will you recognize me, will you kiss me?
I am God's citizen, a staunch believer
in hunger, appetite, and, in His mercy,
fulfilment.
                    Then praise Him for your bread.

Durham bread

Streets of terrace houses cover
the hill, the sun's tufts and hollows
in lilac smoke turning stone
to honey. The railway steps
through on arches. This is Gala
miner and minister, bands that break
lugubrious cries. The hushed brass,
its softly hurled quick touches
a friend's death: yes, I loved you.

Living, like smoke
on stone property, patches of brick
darn a worn fabric, its patch
of small-builders. With stepping
between, a miner,
a lawyer, fragrant and striped
as a cardamom. A tall bird
uncurls its neck
and rises like a figure
off a tarnished penny.
Its streaks of bodily black force
drift at the dun stone
of church architecture.

Some choose not to have
that church. Christ so imbues them,
these workers of Frosterley marble,
their fossil columns, they drop
their Christianity
in heaps of languid clothing
on the river side, swimming until
their bodies with tiredness fill,
naked as the soft opening
they started through.

45

Walking, what I see,
the air lifting between the stepping arches,
is how their spaces
are like the thick slice of Durham bread, cut
against hunger,
slices like generations of boys' mouths,
this boy, Dick, even
now, cramming his
with white, thick unbuttered bread. He feels
that bub, that generative, pert
tenderness of his wife's breasts. His hands
echo her shapes. Durham

bread, as the trains wing it, where
some have neither bread nor love. Slovenly
clothes crease the frail height
of a man buying his stamp,
whose monarch's head removes
a letter to his friend. Take the bread.

(FOR DAVE BELL AND JACKIE LEVITAS)

46

The levels

Past Quaking Houses,
on the bull-neck of the north Pennines, that has no head,
in a flat torn sky,
wind circling among hills, like a miner
with wide shallow bowl, panning –
above Alston, I went with my nets
to dismal grass-blobbed flats, reaching
into the Solway's firth, soft basement
to rubbed, soft water
not poisoned yet by fission, where the fish frisk
in a dismal sort of way. Their tails lash
the brunette forms of the sea.

My nets an impediment over shoulders, catching
at knees, or scraping the back of calf and thigh.
On a journey not so big as a rushlight,
the bog's rushes smeared with sheep's fat,
I went. The quaker graveyard still scythed
of nettle and its remedy, dock. At Silloth
I threw my nets into the sea,
their meshes chagrined with a dead
exposure to air, and no fish.
Nets that weighed on me, hiss in the floating sea.
For hours, against the sea's pull
tugging like any fish's mouth, green flimsy
triangles of salt wrinkling greek characters
on sifting illiterate sand.

At length six fish obliged, as if for pity
flickering over meshes they can't pass. I pulled
them out gasping against the heft
of frigid water, with biting mouths,
scraping upon the element they leave.

And their doleful eyes and breathless gills
tricked of their pasture hang in bodies
laid by on the denser lingual
of a mudded slab.

The silence thickens
and turns to water: lives that bite
the shining levels of mud,
the creamy monstrous air, teeth that gnash it,
are dying. Teeth and eyes hook
with a presentiment of my death.
I have taken your lives –
delicate adroit netsman.

(FOR MICK STANDEN)

A man and a plant in a house

You on a ledge in the sun's co-active
diffusion, with seeds furred
in orange berries, I, with a bed, each capable
of seeding, we start fresh in this house,
being womanless, mutely wailing
continuity and warmth.
But my eyes, these foolish witnesses,
had forgotten those with nothing.

In this room I'm to speak little in, you follow
those gentle battered forms,
your confederate equals, trees the wind sways
open, spreadeagling stormy birds.
Like lace fidelity is lovely
between us. But the flimsy pain of those
I betray, shakiness mine from birth;

for now the modest tender colours weep
at me not strong enough to staunch their blood;
I hear the angels of rebuke, those scratching the glass,
whom I must admit, familiars of dread
sawing ice from a blue pond
for the refrigeration of souls.
I mush perish or speak with them.
In the world, not a leaf is guilty.

Psalmists

She is she who will not come again,
though I ransack the sheets, two canaries

that drop fluttering speech, he,
with his *cantare*, 'two can lie

apart and stay together,' his moist acts
in another's fur. His right of return,

safeguarding in a sac his trailed pubis
frosted in delirium, female with male,

a wing weighted on another's
in mutuality. Here's dense granular night-air,

which is the dead in their marriages,
the silent sifted flesh of wife and man
a granular air, wife husbanding
their love, like honey, like coal
sweet pitchy tar that bubbles understanding,

in front of which this canary and that one

hang from a claw not visible,
translucent howling bear of light,

prairie wind, seen
as a lover's impress on the sheet, wind

swathing wheat, the silk
lying under His unuseful refreshing breath.

*

She has hinged wake-up eyes. They sing
as if for want of bread, that partly-sweet

grain, this before
sugar was born in the mouth.

I praise the God who is marriage.

*

I will feed them, though they never feel
the outside translucent
serene blue. In winter's morning
I leave my house
wedged fragile and large
in Bradford's hills. A concave inverted pond
of blue douses light on me.

*   *

I am a thief. In my hand a piece
of chrome, wrenched
politely off a wrecked car-door. In my other
a windscreen-wiper, that's shucked snow
to rubble, its gums
and teeth crushing
the blade to its brace,
like a flag frozen and adhesive at its staff,
the stiff ribbed droop of its salute.

The wrinkled opals of gas in clay
and water! I break into a lonely man's house
and put my hands
in his airing cupboard. Two birds,
a yellow cinder, like a bangle on the other's neck,
she, dead. In this residence,

this blazing sufficiency of glass,
with one bird's dead life, such inclement unequal
distributed being, I unlearn the worth
of a chrome door-clasp, a blade's pitted
rubber, contused
by its rasping away
of snow.

I steal his yellow oscillating wings.
I will feed and keep alive this male.
My song will learn his, we will both subsist
in societal agitation. The bird is a male harp;
I, David and King, take and strum the lifetimes of his wife.

Apparition

Damage

Is it the top has screwed
from my head, like the cap off a grenade? Screams
rise from me, who's missing my lid. I'll screw
to myself, what I must find again.
He throws the best cup
in the house, not at her; the wall
breaks into china
the handle in pieces dribbles to the skirting.
I've my hands to my ears, to scream,
shaping to a question mark. I am trained
into the serifs, ridges, and hollows of letters;
I am a watermark inside paper. No, I am something;

the boy fastens to the back of the couch
fingers like silent tongues. The voices of father
and mother make of my silence
this question, who will be hurt most?

A man with unclenched fist

They chase about the table, hate, that takes
away gender. Her hair swishing cheeks,
that was the darling of his fingers.

My brother will die of their shouts. He weeps
and I must attend. But why won't they stop, who have
more energy than a child's? Why is this night

different from all others? How can
the four of us, unforced, hold each by the waist
to weep contrition and love? Unlovely mother

and weeping father, divorce, the church's
legal knife. There were chairs and heavenly cups;
a man, with unclenched fist blessed me and vanished;

it was as if I thought I could not die.

Douglas of Sorbie and the adder

In the village of Sorbie a boy called Douglas regularly shared his bowl of porridge with an adder. His mother overheard him speaking to no person she could see, until she finally understood that he was talking with the adder. She called the farm-labourers to destroy the creature, which they did. It is recorded that her child died of grief, and that for many years after children came to garland his grave. This story is recorded in *Tales of Galloway* by Alan Temperley.

A snake mouths a boy's hot gruel – 'move across,
grey beardie.' Over steps, feeling the sun climb
upon darkness, its filaments
filleting tracks with light,
sharing the boy's food an adder raises
its bars and curves of body, a boy
waving a spoon, the snake
a boy's smiling pleasures. The mother

in her pleated skirt watches. We move
in a place of designs, a crust
of gas, and hardened gas, a helix, like chasing
butterflies – or on a concourse
where stars lash, and play,
and fall, like a chain of bracelet, on a kitchen-
table, each month. Abandon, or the spokes
of a wheel plugged to the hub, like us,
formed for work?
Would stars rive out another's gravity
collapsing the life, to make a lesser system?
For less work, would we?

The mother, her ovum, her twist of feckless gene,
watches her child touch a snake, she
infatuated with his future – a pleated
sun success opens, who will give her child

to Georgian London, anachronistic
huge casual brutalities, the houses laid
along grasses and a resting sickle.
The double-breasted widths of the rich
swarm in fine worsted.

She tip-toes, her moulded thighs swish to barns
where day-labourers thresh: 'Fetch hoes,' she says.
A snake is harmed. A boy screams, piecing
the dead flesh, a snake's papery
eyes bathed in venom, the evil's counterbalanced
justifying hesitant smiles of 'let him,'
from hired men, like entropic stilled planets.
'I will eat grass'
he tells his mother.

Her totemic sculpture that swoons one face
above another. His will faints in hers.
He whets a spoon against the slab
a snake bit to shed its poison, like taking
stamens from a crocus mouth
to sweeten bread. The soft selfless gullet of sunrise takes
his grief and intelligence.

Children who are friends, and friends
who did not know him, garland his marker,
discomfited, petal-spears pieced to
a day's tufted eye. A sister says,
'Michael I must take you home, mother is just now
putting up the lamp.'

Galloway's religious killings, and the lonely language of Gaelic

The tide woke, lifting our estuary mud
the Solway tasted – river, like a fish, sucked
it in, hated the taste it vented, but slowed
as salt and mist kindled the Machar's breast.

In neither fresh or salt a stake rises;
Wigtown's to drown a girl. 'Oh recant,'
we beg. No, she was sorry. Gently
we pull, and with her religious hair
tie her to a pole. The flower struggles,

twisting her rims with the invisible
fearful moon's untwisting a flint-hued
watery skein, that billows her dress,
and steps above her,

whose gasping delicately fills me. Not the clash
of her precentor's psalm;
or the miscegenation
of her people's voices with his. Her 'sorry'
is mist in our windows' cavities,
not in our Gaelic, but the tuned
bitter second tongue, not our flickering schwa

but speaking in English, of her clothed form
on a sea bed (my daughter's face
fine and lone as hers). We speak

of a girl's *christe eleison*, the chants of pain
her panting, breath, bubbles smashing in air,
not acts to heft in Gaelic's lofty storage.

For weight our tongue with crime, in its over-plus
of delicacy, its lyric the tussle
of a lonely language demented

with heroes, burden it with our crime,
and Gaelic, the gentle immaculate tongue dies.
But English, frequent shit in its grass, puts spears

of lilac seed through the matted crime.
Their mind's broken lightning in each fuzz
of soft-spoken seed commuting to earth

the generations of its success.

I ask the depths of hill snow, Who will be brave again?

I read in Alan Temperley's *Tales of Galloway* that, in the period of the Covenanters,
Wigtown pleaded with two women to recant their faith or die. They would not do so,
and the two were tied to stakes set in the estuary and left for the tide. Galloway is a
complex historical area and it is nearly impossible to separate out the Scots and Irish
components, although the term Galloway Irish is far from being a fiction. About a
hundred and seventy years previously Gaelic was spoken in south-west Scotland, and I
suppose, in the poem, that the population indigenous to Wigtown and its surrounding
area spoke Gaelic first and then English. I am not sure to what extent correspondence
between language and race existed, or if it could ever have been determined.

The silence

As I close my eyes, I can see
the village and its plan, askant
my line of vision. Tilt this, one melts
to its plan; lift, the village is
in one piece, its existing life
from limestone, its diagram a street
in which no car dare pass
another. A donkey's ambling width.

As I pass, their stare catches me
by the shoulder, their shadows gone still
as a lizard in flight changes
the lines of its short, tailless life
into a radiating mass of lines waving
frail limbs and feet on stone.
All stone cracks, all
cracks form lizards. No sawn blocks
but rock scooped, as a natural
prison is. No grass, or tree
through which a bee treads
its shadow, counterfeit
of self, over the leaf-blades.
Man, animal and woman stand
stripped of shadow among the stone;
its pargeting flaky
as a blister dried to its face.
I stare at my palms, their milky
abrasions, the pale veins
in the wrist, the whitened
character and life-lines.

Sea and rock
caught together in a concurrence
of stone and tons of soft salt force,
the trapped unshadowed
sea in anguish. These faces
break their alien stare on me. I'm the same,
all skin and body, my shadow
buried in their stone. Lord God,

I am a bit of the sea:
I don't believe in you.

Gifts

In medio ramos annosaque bracchia pandit
Ulmus opaca ingens, quam sedem somnia volgo
Vana tenere ferunt foliisque sub omnibus haerent.

VIRGIL, *AENEID*

A sunk plot, in this city,
of nurseries: the herbs, flowers
and branched forms moistened
in their warmed sections. I stare
at what will shed
sugary plums. 'Take it' – smiling –
'and plant its union
of stock and scion four inches
above soil.' In this spring
where breath is distinguishable
from thin smoke only in
its having no scent,
no sweet, destructive odour of cell
in flames, I took
the tree, disentangling
roots, easing from the tuft of struggling forms
feet, the bituminous soil
in soft morsels.

By May, flowers: their hue
wings of bees, their exposed parts
a sly feed sucked by a head
with winged legs.
Latched in the shed, implements with
teeth to the wall, their grainy poles
smudged with sweat,
the pale wood softened

in winter's blotch. Wasps
held by raised wings bite
out fallen plums.

Winds streaked with cold lift
branches, as a girl stepping
from water switches her hair.
Fixed in the skins of plums held
to the leaf-backs, dots of pink
fleck and gather, like fish
in chevrons of water. Winds dissolve,
the raised and half-raised branches
disentangle and hang
the hard fruits dripping sugars.
Tawny persuasions of light
on leaf and skin.
Smeltings of a sugary sun, the soft
succulent feeders:
for which I meant to use you like a slave.

Forgive the trespass
of my hands in your leaves;
your barren presence, if it comes to that,
I will leave standing in this sugary sun,
its mildews, its hoar.

Semite

(my name is Ratcliff. Why do they pull it apart as if I were a Jew?)

'Ratcliff.' What did he mean, to rile
my name? The school screws seven to a bench.
Lap, works the tongue. Cutlery
stinks lightly of metal polish. I lade jam.
In a great hall at war shortages
cry out for silent heroisms. Fingers
of food-stained wood tighten their flowering
in intricate desire on lozenges
of lilac glass. 'Rat-cliff?' As if
I'd pissed me-sel', or that his soft-eyed pleading
that mocked my hauteur, since I'm of the south,
was not enough to make his fellow-cogs
lifting knives of jam howl.

*

She married dark hair. Margaret hoped to see
her face raised on the water's medal, in
the well, but she got me: a child.
Long thighs, long fingers – a skein of time's
cottony dangling. We bud a stem
too dried to make a child. Her whimpering ceased.
A d & c took it from her. This one,
darlin', I say, the next is yours.

Blasts of black smoke. The city unpeels
a burning fetid tyre's softening forms.
Conscience softens. We're slivers
off the Metropolitan Railway's carriage axles.
It's hard to be unimportant: harder,
she says,
to be conscienceless.

Constancy eased marriage. In earlier solitude
I formed the lips of friendship, kissed
the glass, and made nothing. I,
a brand-new kid, came in my fingers: howled.
Were I a cat, its gender cut from it,
my fur pattable with need, and soft,
I'd roll in dust letting it sift in me
and better every life of mine I have.

*

I dreamed of constancy. A hill
spreading a field curved in an s-shape to
a stream withered with pebble. A bank
of earth and boulders, behind it
our dead; a cat, a tree, a woman tearing
soft hazel nuts into her mouth.
The land mists, the furrows spun off
the blade so deeply, they hair this corduroy.
This sighting along England, critical
of it. I see what I shan't have, women
with their quick. Between its teeth, then,
death took me, but dropped my mind, a bone,
litter for a small fold of earth. In this
subtle field of England, I drown,
streaking, hissing
in the flecked candied flints. My fingers
turn something that's light and sheens, not
swart pebbles pressed to the eyes
to see inside the world, sight and opacity
making vision, but a matt unslithering
oblong of glass, transparency, thinness
I drag two fingers on preparatory
to setting it with the slicks of spit
in a microscope – the father's gift I broke
before I'd used it. In my mind this time
no breaking; constancy is clarity.

A mottled green drifts in the glass; is it
our constancy, through which her character
stains my new-found conduct?

*

We both, in two. A head butting, a fish,
splutters in her, but scared of too much sea,
of that authentic element. Of any.
I am a Jew, who claims his English form
is bogus, a self the candle's flame
envelopes, with a flame standing within,
pleading its dignity; some christians
abhor the temporary miracle:
a constant dew-shaped form, holding both flames.
Dew weeps, and the self vanishes. I aspired
to a fair-headed saxon elegance.

*

A Jew is teaching Poles Yiddish. They will
use it as part of their language, a part
of Polish (of Poland), as expiation
and scapegoat – mixed tallows that point
a single fluttering, with every part
of the soft pennant, this flimsy orange cloth
sure of extinction. Should this be?
The letters are Hebrew, many of the words
German, with ash in their chests' tangled widths.
Brush it off. It can be brushed off.

They'd better hurry. No Jews will be in Poland
to speak it with. I burn, my heat a deft
clumsy mismanaged constancy. My body
like chalk on a blank patient slate. I cover it,
and her as well,
with words that vein with a substance proper to
their innocence. I find the hard word, hope.

Polish fragments of dust

(between Poles and Jews of Poland)

'Too many to hide.' With flimsy rage
we climbed into the hiding-places you created
and showed to the Germans, your occupiers.
We hid in coral, in the helix of shells. True?
In ovens, rain-casks, in the water
lithe and forgiving, in mothy folds of camphored linen,
in others' beds: no –
in soiled clothing, in the chambers
of gas,
in the spaces of our *absentia*.

*

We dance-stumble in the cellars, fingers
softening our fontanelles to baby's blood.

Children pick the struggling hermit-crabs, and you,
with Germans, take from their sockets rooted stars,
the earthy sky in dark concaves, rock-pools,
these gymnasia of survival.

*

In Polish snow, she lightly touches a German:
'one pistol between five Jews. Who wouldn't
kill those we hate, like you?'
In the moon's biting halo, two humans
white as gathered moths.

Can loathing and accusation be gentle
as a cat that noses the spaces of balustrades?
The poem's language, but the verse's burden.

You desire ships, your scudding power
with its unceasing speech, that inward stammer.
They bucket teeming seas. They'd be carriages
on land, dipping through hollows, stuffed
with Polish berries, the little blueberries
that have no scent, and break the heart.

*

To ask to live is blameless. Your ships,
their machinery is frosted echoes
I bite through. You are Sebastians
and Christian infantry
with arrows in your flesh, as they are
in our quarrelsome bodies, which are homeless, too,
as sin disremembered.

Freedom clings to you like a shirt in holes,
a wet flimsy headless shirt. My Polish
soil, my Polish Polish air, Poland
touch our ghosts with care, they will scream all day,
and you'll be in tears for ever, whole angels
in the religious skies, where they use
the time for petitions of injured souls.

Yet on earth destiny cries out, kisses you.

Now cross the ice in bliss and peace.

Tangled in war

In Stornoway a shack, two stanchions by it that drip
the news of war. In this stub of tower,
tongued vertical planks
under a glaze chipped like nail-varnish, homely Norwegian
smokes on faded wood, a language
that the storm, which suffers its force,
aches to mate with. Our sword, the hilt
a dragon sinuous as vine,

is better-made than any sightly implements
the farm uses, that Viking ship
billowing between the glen's flanks, its tree-mast
a head of clustered antler. Christ torn in it.

Everything is war. The share is beaten back
into a sword, the storm is a house
that splinters it. I feel
the house's beds of child-birth linen, its tenderness
daughters' exile in cities, cunning in exile.
Theirs is the child-freshness. My hands lie
in the house's space like a wound, its innocence
a past woven as a thicket into its present.
The shadows blood like thorn.

Linked by their acts

Up through a field of stone fissure the gentians' pudgy
    blossom
made from parts
of bodies, a cheek
kissed, kneecaps, the noses
of assassins. Where crannied hills
skip in God's smiling like lambs, these flowers
light death's route. We, the first fingerings of spring,
would make couples of ourselves. The half-ounce
of scorpion un-nerves us. Its pebble
oval like an eye.

What hankering translucent forms? It is early ghosts,
the man, a dog snuffing
urine, a wonky nail splayed on a fence;
its kidney shape concentrates
in the dog's left medulla. Like a fish he tightens
the leash rubbing his sodden master's wrist.
Oh oh.
A bleb on the dog's thigh. A man chooses
you will die, thin alpine-pink hair. The crab
in your thigh. Peace to you.

The linked plod of eventual ghosts,
for after death
memory makes spirits of us
to asperge our beings. It touches
Emmanuel, the God waiting in us.
Memory, like the wind that jolts open the heads of trees,
and swells them, memory, like the aureole of a woman's
    breast,
that transmits care and stiffens the nipple,
its deluge of milk,

memory touching sprigs of hopping Juniper
put from Noah's ship of wood,
memory, its web of instinct, strong as sex
and more greatly innocent. Like nuts honey splinters
and pieces together, memory like halva,
memory a nimbus rainy with its moon
in our illusion of its tenderness.
This dog leashed to his sodden master.
So much happens in the sky.

Jews without Arabs

Did we make them leave, did they turn the wheel
of dispersion? We flee
through desert prairie, those grasses
that never flower, though the cold at night
is the thought of the day's herbage
glimpsed in heat. Where are they, and the grasses?
They left, as if
we were boys to be shunned, without our sex,
miniature unicorns, but flatteringly;
like guano, like the bats' cave.
Their absence is our loneliness.
A fan full circle. If we stepped
into our shadow, we'd have no breath.

Here is a provision of bread the sun bakes,
a space in rock hiding Moses
God seeks to kill. We're Jewish Pharoahs
flicking water, whipping it. Canute's deathless stick
that parts the sea – fringed with Sinai's bog-cotton,
its flags of small dissension. All soldiers,
weapons, manuals, sweethearts
in kodak, sink, with the claws of a tank's tread
and the howling metal roar.
Ezekiel has bitter signs: in the lilac sky
his wheel turns
its inner circle in reverse. I free a soldier

like a fly, into desert meadows
of pebble, pale and fine as sugar. 'Unacceptable,'
in delicate abandon
in fine shunning wings, the mayfly cries.
She, the humming-bird's constant intrepid companion.
Theirs the mixed family of creation.

Our enemy's absence, which is the spear of loneliness,
an undying son we each have,
the unimaginable, unsought-for child
with us by a sandy spring, where we substantiate
our constant debarment – it mutely hammers
the dreaming part of our lives: a bruise, an inescapable
panic of inseparable pain.
The milk in our mouths is burnt for ever.
Friends, friends, what may we change to?

Secret Service

(between a Jew, visiting, and a police agent)

We meet by Ovid's grave
exile its greening, its tree, lament.
I slough off my boots
and rest my back against it. The tears
distant as thunder. His suit light-weight
as skin, 'brother,' he says
and gives me a *Genesis* in Hebrew.

Lemberg 1825, sisal knotted on each signature,
its end-papers eau-de-nil
and torn. He eyes me delicately. The book
warped, as if under a stone
in raucous swivelling sea-water,
with, in indelible ink, 'Issac Elias.'

*

He takes two strides, 'I'm a Jew,' (he tells me)
'so I give you this.' And 'brother,'
as if he knew
I knew no Jew was in him. He prays
in Hebrew, him and me in the synagogue
of the Sephardim, me silent.

The prayers fold back in their books, Jews' smiles and
    hooked fingers.
Theirs is the feast – thimbles of spirit
and half-sweet cakes. We caress him
with Jews' morsels.

It is Family Family: an aunt
prints lips on a ten-year-old's
brow rising a forest of blond hay.
The air, the skin smells
of youth abandoned.

*

Jew and Colonel. He stares, and, with his thinking
transforms me. I've the fuselage of a mouse
and hooked wings: me, bat-like
in his Transylvania, his packed sentinel of conifer.
'Warn the Jew to be no Jew,' their aphoristic murmur.

He spits on me; this sud, a vaccine
of Jew, puffed like ash into the blood.
'Inoculate a Jew with some Jew; he'll be no Jew.'
Oh he knew, this client
of Hebrew.

Oh, oh, yes yes, Issac you indeed
is it, in indelible ink?

*

In the spaces between God's star-like fingers
with wings slatted either side of my flesh;
with these crooked battens, these bones of fragile evil
that trellis the sun's wrathful face,
my form whizzes home
crinkling like a zip, or a rack wound
upon its cog. Which breaks my back's
listless ease
with my wife's welcome I'm not worthy to receive.
She spreads angels arms
jagged and wing-like. 'Elias,' she shrieks

in the Hebrew I've none of. With her small
hand-embosser she gave me, I impress
my name in fear
the investigators will come
upon me, in Hebrew.

Wait for me, I say.
And I wait for you, 'my sweet perfumed self,'
you tell me as I lean over you.
This earth of wives and ashes.
And fear and defeat soused with sweetness and love.

The hand's black hymns

In August I began to love you.
Two islands, yours a scorpion stinging
in sea's acid, a divine, consistent, serene
blue fluid to the sky's.
In my fields of poppy separation undrowses me,
flowers' deaf phones, their veins twitching
oblivion, mouthpieces of an incontinence
brine rubs through. In their tidal roots
distance rocks each land, and separates both.
Distance is smiling. Faithful

as air, where are you? Or is this
presumptuous? In tufted forests I wander a finger
discharging its senses in maidenhair.
Less flexible than building-steel, wind
bonds to this island form: its Roman word, its lost
Roman meaning, *vectis, vector*. Innocent
stinging messenger, I follow you like
wind its message. Poppies rummage wheat. Because
I want you, are you less absent?

My hand's a member, a clover's flower
in waiting. 'I can touch you (I say)
you, who lie in the next room.' I say what
deceives pain. It's our voices mate, by phone.
Japanese terrain, the ochre-skin, toad-smooth
hue of the stung creature, in lulling acid,
the scorpion, its lovely innocent head;
and this island the springs tether,
its inner brain the sea wrinkles – is 'venture.'

Our airmail: yes, sweet, we live off the trees
made thin. Refugees are like dust, and all
we bear is absence. Please, put out your hand, if
you touch me, I can. Yes, love, yes

the airmail paper on which we sigh
grins at the words, my fountain-pen that tugs
black hymns from its crushed reluctant sheet. Your fingers
hold the poem, your idolatrous desire
perfects mine. The hand
that reads the poem is more beautiful than it.

Mr Lloyd's life

Being a child, I moved with Mr Lloyd
slow, his leg taken in an earlier war, and reached
the others,
each equal as the next, like flies. That war rose
half translucent, like a cliff
the flesh of soldiers
dashed on it.

'A great day for the race.' His joke cultivated
laughter, like flowers heaped
over more, on wood, a joke bestowed,
asked every day, a child's man the wars hurt still.
'What race, sir?' Lloyd's boys who walked by him,
his legs covering earth
in another war, instructed
to have an answer. 'The human race,' Lloyd said.

Men gassed and watched, suffered the children.
We waited to be destroyed, the gasser pressing naked eyes
at the chamber's aperture. In goes
his vision, through the lucid Jacob-glass.
Lloyd's hand easing his thigh
in equal paces, in pain, as I now understand,
learning to take English, from a good man,
tender as Shakespeare,
in both wars, their midsts, moving from the hips
that could bear him.

I watch this war. It is another's blood is poured,
as if I came to die
and stiffen. Under the feet of children raging
with distance, he lays the fire of Welsh hills
that have cooled to grass and milk.

To a lighthouse

After years I turned home, self-hatred
shredding my leaves, my feet huge
as a horse-chestnut's leaf, dray, clydesdale
useless for loads. How I forfeited self
with hatred, how I stabbed it over
and planned death;

for to have deceived
the self, was to make a shyster
of the body's innocence. So I tricked
my mind to accept murder
from me. 'If you wish,' the mild being's
shy smile shook the spine-pole of messages.

I pictured my head in a landscape, jigsawed
the whole, the skull shimmering
from its environs, bony hills, with trees
pinning them. And if you looked,
a hare, huge and electric, earth's force
transfixing her.

At the back of my head, blue soil, me, inching
timid suicide.
The method: to take the body
from embraces, an angel's even;
the means and cause: fear of wings. And search
for hope, a lichen, such as you might enjoy
to find trees murmuring with? No.

This resort of ships, my home.
Between the privacies of break-water I fed
self hatred, as I was fed
madness and seaweed, left by coward tides

cinched round earth, moon's bitter, ungraspable
girdle. Subject to jigging water,
I, a sad, lonely man, licensed
between home and marina, entered a boat, clacking
the heads of nails that pierce the slippy planks.

Happy, ever after, to run
for the lighthouse blinking
its existence. Until one
comes and sledges out its light, those pupils,
élèves of light, disciples, disciplines
of guidance, and trust. O the dear blank eyes.
They have not done it yet. They think to.

Pity, a machine-gun huffing
air, swivels from me.

When I showed the townspersons
jasper, in a cube I had lifted
from waves tossed wide as dead arms,
they commended
the self-interest,
that had
stooped to find it in milky waves,

this cubed apostle, this quartz learning
from godhead to be impure. I rejoiced,
who will not pawn
the cubed jasper. Or if
I did, I'd lose my mind, as much
as a wave looses its hand
on pebble, oolite, hematite, the teeth
of granite gliding molten pools: the belligerence
and splendour of a form.

I think of marble. The dark waves
in it are Masons flitching the town's market;
the white, bird's guano, is youth
voided after their labour; they mewl
bitched tears.

Lord, you should have inserted
your ghostly hand between sperm and egg
in the sanctuary of a woman's body, to prevent
me. I am a gem-collector's stony
tit of facts.

The land tips squares of quartz.
Prong, here, the theodolite's
three legs, spy in its protractor
the scythe of its heterodox
gaze, Ireland and Kintyre,
kingdoms of the Gaels' sad dipthongs,
language a gull hovers
of shadow on a wave.

The lighthouse keeper tags a
bird, its barbed flight in his beating mind.
My feet, clop
on cubes of stone, under the beacon's
other side of night, blinking
constant vision. Mr Donald lets me
lie in darkness as the light sits up,
washes, shines the self, is trustworthy.

First a craftsman's solitude made
lantern, then lenses. Mr Donald says
they are bullseyes. Only the light shoots them
rubbed in oil
on diamonds to get consistency
of vision;

stupendous, brighter than day, to guide
ships through
a sour cringe of providence and waves.

Ships fleeing
between nations,

swishing the furred indigoes
of oil on waving crabs.
This performance, its entirety.
Speckled cancerous herring, a dark-footed
sun, prancing upon sea. Now I will save my life
in my hand.

Decent God, you need our love, as all
need, helping you through bleak necessities
of love's exchange. Or else, a lonely smashed God
a gull's ambiguous death, in rigging
a feathery casualty: a broken angel: one of yours.

Lens-breakers

Wood ash stinks a cat's fur, sweeter than smoke, wood
cut, hovers a scent like chyle or sweet vomit. Fire,
in the wedges, hides in smoky quadrants of agate.
Ash sugars the cat; his wedge-head with arrowy fangs,
eyes half-closed pebble. His mineral
distant gaze is topaz. Fierce and red
in the lap, hunger turned us up for his
thin lucid fire to be fed.

Since I'm mad, approximately, I yearn
to be kind to some creature. Our cottage hawthorn
leans on, its grime of white smelt
in petals. The meadow sprays red-currant, apple,
dusty plums, echoing the tides' salt. You can't
be sure it's brine or sugars
dotting the skin. From the sea I picked a cube
of jasper like a turquoise fly.

A track of scurf (I mean the reader
no harm by this) shakes, slowly,
to the point, that empties from its throat cubes
of pink granite; below, this bitter ship,
Deutschland. Its wrecking tries faith in their God;
if the spiky fingers are like splintered
arms, their arms are fingers.

Lloyds pays. Many nights of one episode redeem
the dear bonds. But nostrils do not now
bubble air through brine. Once I lulled a cat
whose nose spluttered blood, a car hit. Lloyds
pays, and charges rise to honour the future.

My love, I'm saying men
step off a truck, whose half-haul
tarpaulin hoops to a stop, handing sledges
to each other, like buddies consigned
to courage in war, bringing the lantern
to earth, with mercury vapour behind
reflecting dutiful glass that twists each scrap
of wandering light through the lenses rasped
on laps, in water and oil, until the bits
rubbed into the lens comprise
a consistent vision.

They wedge at a sledgeable angle, and splinter
the eyes, like a peacock's feathers' eyes, their alert
serene mercury heating to a chlorophyll
in a leafy beam of fifteen miles,
that cannot see. The light flutters
like a butterfly, I'm sure.

On hammers, blistered glass.
The ostrich digests iron; the loch's
wary salt shunts glass under it. The lighthouse
wears no eyes.

If I'm petulant, I'll bash sea-shells
on the difficult track threading to the sea: no way,
no way, my wife, cats, my smashed
decibels. The lenses have their ghosts tripped
from Edinburgh. When electric quits
(it quits) the ships wreck, and raise costs.
So it goes, a trinity, of ships
insurance, failed light;

the lantern, the strophe hammered apart, the hymn, the
   Jupiter-eyes
beaten thin as air-mail paper.
The men of divine darkness, spattered with drunk vomit
after their work. Tools
lean in the corners of housing.

Honouring the father

A river town presses moonlit circles
from fish-shells, buttons for blouse and shirt
sex separates by gender. I am grass
whose seed crams with broken-up lightning,
procreation's lilac forms,
eyes dropping through earth. We are confederate grasses.
The wind bending us is God's sequence of hands
whose leafless transit gives us birth, turning
to nothing.

It is a question of seed, as the moth stubs
its life into the charred light.
My love, my parent, my moth rest
a little, father, your rubbed generous lightning,
you, ageing magnificent sovereign.
Is it permitted to touch you? You have
your father's life I have been allowed
of lilac fluttering chromosomes.
All night the shop is open, with its eyes and lilies.
The candles bloom with moth and daisy.
Come a little this way, I pray you.

Cleaning the light

My father sits by the screen, each of six contestants
made foolish with knowledge. The compère smiling
at a woman's naked shoulders
and timid gentle mouth, his body between pulsing wings
is absent, the mind
beating in its bodilessness.

Father thrusts his merciful beak-like head
and light hair, which is beautiful;
the screen cannot receive
father. 'Oh you fool, you clown,'
he shouts at the bodiless form.

A ferocious light unspent in winter's branches,
barbaric, judgmental, orange
distinct over the bark; it is this world
and his mind at it. Like a lighthouse-man
fastened outside to the lantern
and its beams of light, a broom swathed
in a torn overall, shoving off moth-like clinging snow
suffusing dark in the lantern's octagonal glass.

It is praising light to clean
a bare harsh existence
of the spring-like dark. Such my father,
his retinal intelligence.

Tenderness

Not trusted with a key, I jar the front-door's lock,
its nice prevention held in my parents' hands.
A woman in the hall points flowers, scent and tungsten
showing grime in the tiles, their earth-hued triangles
of trunk, of bough, fruit and blossom making a tree.
The house is my parents' sanctuary,
therein
the woman, our hall's solicitous familiar,
like an oyster-catcher jabbering
a red bill for her endangered young.

My parents form a pearl
fit to pass through a space, to hold the staying loop
for blouse and shirt. May I touch you both?
We cannot touch. We speak of ships scudding to Palestine,
male Jews and passionate rigid women hoping
we will connect. We have wasted
our lives, waiting for tenderness.

My parents, my lovers, pour the tea
and let the swollen belly of pewter cool. The shop will stay
    open,
like a bulging lamp,
a topaz ossuary, its jovial thick-set beams
fuelled by the dead. The light feels barbaric,
this quiet rape of darkness,
a moth's wings clapping itself into life
that burns up right away.

Father, mother, your moth-like lives are never spent,
waiting for tenderness,
the nape of the neck will be kissed.

Fathers

My father's determination
was to be ash. With my
mother's submission
he is burned. 'Yes
Ash that is not
like thread, or snow' she said.
In her
like nothing.

But that is kindness. I opened
a box. A dead mother
had limpeted a green
blue globe of thread
to the wood,
like mould, which
as I touched, her
glistening kids volted
from, colonizing the white
piny zone, leaving
the father's spiny fibres, by her
chewed to gossamer,

his consubstantial self in her dry diligence

the father my ignorant
finger made dust of.